Polar Bears

Victoria Blakemore

For Jacob and Dylan, my cousins who love to read

Copyright info/picture credits

Cover, Storyblocks; Page 3, kloster21/Pixabay; Page 5, skeeze/Pixabay; Page 7, michaklootwijk/AdobeStock; Page 9, Patrick Poendl/AdobeStock; Pages 10-11, Gunnar/AdobeStock; Page 13, StockSnap/Pixabay; Page 15, tpsdave/Pixabay; Page 17, bernswaelz/Pixabay; Page 19, Godot13/WikimediaCommons; Page 21, skeeze/Pixabay; Page 23; BDougherty/Pixabay; Page 25, skeeze/Pixabay; Page 27, raekreis/Pixabay; Page 29, kdsphotos/Pixabay; Page 31, onkelramirez1/Pixabay; Page 33, Storyblocks

Table of Contents

What are Polar Bears?   2

Size   4

Physical Characteristics   6

Habitat   8

Range   10

Diet   12

Communication   16

Movement   18

Polar Bear Cubs   20

Polar Bear Life   22

Lifespan   24

Population   26

Polar Bears in Danger   28

Helping Polar Bears   30

Glossary   34

What Are Polar Bears?

Polar bears are large mammals. They are the largest kind of bear.

They are known for their large size and the white color of their fur. It works as **camouflage** in their icy habitat.

Polar bears are **apex predators** in their habitat. They are at the top of the **food chain** and have no natural predators.

Size

Polar bears are often between six and nine feet long from nose to tail.

They usually weigh between 600 and 1,400 pounds. Some may even grow to weigh over 1,700 pounds.

Male polar bears are usually
larger than female polar bears.

Physical Characteristics

Polar bears have a thick layer of fat under their skin. It is called blubber and it helps to keep them warm.

Their long neck and narrow head make them very **streamlined**. They can move quickly through the water.

Polar bear fur is **transparent**. It looks white because there is so much of it. Underneath the fur, their skin is actually black. It **absorbs** heat.

Habitat

Polar bears are usually found on the tundra or on sea ice. They prefer areas around the **coast** where they can more easily find prey.

They are excellent swimmers and often swim miles away from shore to find new patches of sea ice.

Range

Polar bears are found in the Arctic Circle. It is the area of land and ocean around the North Pole.

They are found in places like Canada, Russia, Alaska, and Greenland.

Diet

Polar bears are **carnivores**. They eat meat. Their diet is made up of seals, fish, birds, and young walruses. Their sharp claws help them to catch their prey.

Polar bears have also been known to eat berries and plants such as kelp when they are unable to find other food.

Polar bears eat seals because they have a lot of fat. The fat provides polar bears with enough **calories** to survive in the cold.

Polar bears hunt by themselves. They often look for holes or cracks in the ice because it may mean that there are seals nearby.

Prey can be hard to find. Polar bears can travel long distances before they catch anything.

Arctic foxes often follow polar

bears when they are hunting. The

Arctic foxes eat their leftovers.

Communication

Polar bears use scent, sound, and movement to communicate with each other. They have a scent they use to mark their **territory**. It tells other bears to stay away.

Movements like head wagging can show that a polar bear wants to play.

Polar bears can hiss, snort,

chuff, and growl. A deep

or loud growl shows anger.

Movement

Polar bears have been known to run up to twenty-five miles per hour. This is when **sprinting**. They usually walk at about three or four miles per hour.

Their paws have fur on them. This helps them to stay warm on the ice. It also keeps them from slipping.

Polar bears are good swimmers.

Their front paws are a bit

webbed, which helps them to

swim. Their blubber helps them

to float. **19**

Polar Bear Cubs

Polar bears have up to three babies, or cubs.

Before polar bear cubs are born, their mothers build a den in the snow and ice. The den helps to keep the mother and cubs safe and warm for the first few months.

Cubs stay with their mother for just over two years. They learn how to hunt, swim, and survive.

Polar Bear Life

Polar bears are usually solitary. They spend most of their time alone.

Most polar bears do not **hibernate** like other bears. Only mothers do when they are in their dens with their cubs.

Polar bears can be very **aggressive**. They may fight with other bears or attack humans.

Lifespan

Polar bears often live between twenty and twenty-five years in the wild. They have been known to live as long as thirty-two years.

They are fully grown and able to have cubs by the time they are four or five years old.

Population

Polar bears are listed as **vulnerable**. They are close to becoming **endangered**. Their population is **declining**.

There are thought to be fewer than 25,000 polar bears left in the wild.

Many polar bears are also kept

in zoos around the world.

Polar Bears in Danger

The main threat that polar bears face is rising temperatures. The sea ice that they rely on for hunting is melting.

Many polar bears are being forced to go farther inland to find food.

Polar bears are having a hard time finding enough food. They are also in danger of conflict when they get close to humans.

Many people know about the problems that polar bears face and are trying to help.

They want to try to stop the change in temperature so that polar bear habitats are not destroyed.

There are laws that protect polar bears from being hunted. Only the Inuit people are allowed to hunt polar bears.

Another way people are trying to help is through research. They hope that knowing a lot about polar bears will allow us to help them more.

Glossary

Absorb: to take in

Aggressive: mean, unfriendly, ready to fight

Apex predator: the top predator in the area

Calories: units of energy

Camouflage: using color to blend in to the surroundings

Carnivore: an animal that eats only meat

Coast: the area where land meets the ocean

Declining: getting smaller

Endangered: at risk of becoming extinct

Food Chain: a sequence that shows how each living thing gets food

Hibernate: when an animal sleeps through the winter

Sprinting: running at top speed

Streamlined: smooth, rounded surface that allows for fast movement through water

Territory: an area an animal claims as its own

Transparent: letting light pass through

Vulnerable: an animal that is likely to become endangered

Webbed: joined by a web

About the Author

Victoria Blakemore is a first grade

teacher in Southwest Florida with a

passion for reading.

You can visit her at

www.elementaryexplorers.com

Also in This Series

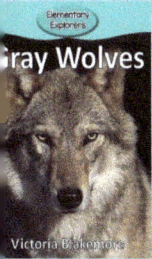

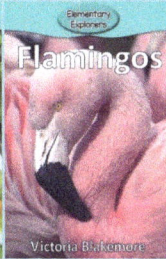

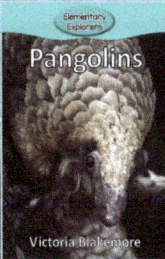

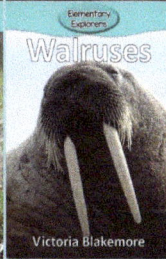

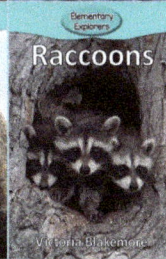

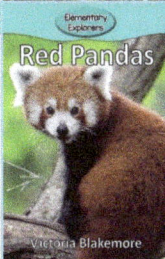

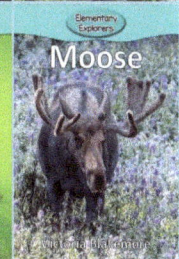

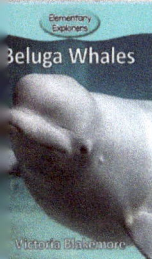

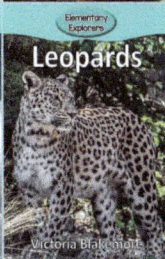

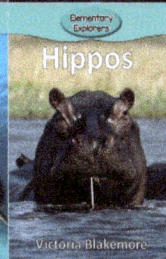

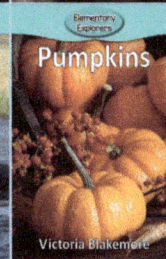

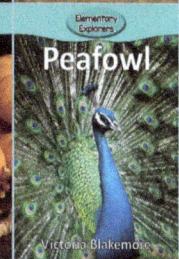

Gray Wolves	Sloths	Flamingos	Camels	Koalas	Honey Bees
Pandas	Pangolins	White-Tailed Deer	Orcas	Giraffes	Corn
Meerkats	Echidnas	Walruses	Raccoons	Bald Eagles	Apples
Arctic Foxes	Red Pandas	Cassowaries	Tigers	Ladybugs	Moose
Beluga Whales	Leopards	Elephants	Jellyfish	Binturongs	Lions
Dolphins	Reindeer	Hammerhead Sharks	Hippos	Pumpkins	Peafowl

Elementary Explorers

Victoria Blakemore

Also in This Series

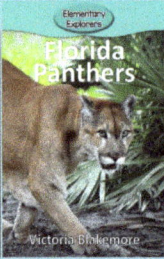

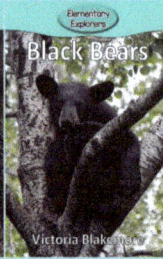

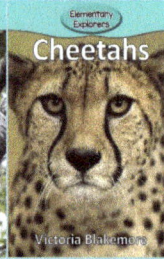

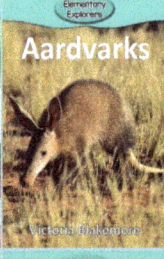

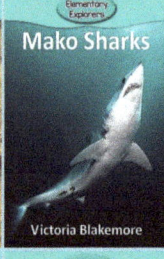

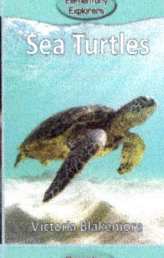

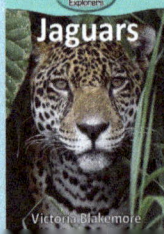

Chameleons	Florida Panthers	Aye-Ayes	Black Bears	Cheetahs	Manatees
Gingerbread	Polar Bears	Hot Chocolate	Orangutans	Coyotes	Marshmallow
Strawberries	Aardvarks	Mako Sharks	Alligators	Frogs	Hedgehog
Brown Bears	Bongos	Sea Turtles	Quokkas	Muskrats	Zebras
Red Foxes	Ring-Tailed Lemurs	Platypuses	Anteaters	Kangaroos	Rhinos
Jaguars	Wombats				

Victoria Blakemore

www.ingramcontent.com/pod-product-compliance
Lightning Source LLC
Chambersburg PA
CBHW051253020426
42333CB00025B/3186